MIGRATIONS

An Almanac for the Soul

JACQUI BONWELL
ANDY CAHILL

D1523078

INTRODUCTION

My name is Jacqui Bonwell. I'm a yoga teacher and motivational speaker, and I've devoted my life to serving people at the place of their deepest need so they can reach their greatest dreams.

And my name is Andy Cahill. I'm a personal transformation coach, and I help people leverage their own inner creativity to live bold and joyful lives.

This journal reflects the insights and questions that have had the most impact in our lives and the lives of those we serve. Every human, no matter where we stand, wrestles with desire, doubt, and despair. We long for what we don't have. We doubt we will ever get it. We despair when we've lost it. In all cases, we lose sight of the simple truth that all we really have is right now. This moment alone is where we live and where we act.

Great wisdom traditions throughout history have recognized this. Life is never static. It is always in flux. A dynamic, cyclical interplay between all things. Push and pull. Yin and yang. Light and the shadow. Joy and suffering. Birth and death. All of it coming together, right here, right now. We cannot run from it, no matter how much we might want to. We are always in this moment. Even choosing to do nothing is a choice that shapes our now.

The only real choice is to lean in. To say yes to life in every moment, whatever it offers. To join in the unending dance of the seasons, all life migrating through it. It is from that place that you can act from your deepest truth.

This journal was written to help you do just that. There are 108 questions and idea to meditate on, spread out over six seasons: Spring, Summer, Fall, Hurricane Season, Winter, and back around to Spring again. Jacqui has devoted much of her life to studying the Yoga Sutras, and the prompts are numbered in the same chapter-and-verse fashion (1.1, 1.2, 1.3... etc). There is plenty of space to write your thoughts and insights along the way, and we invite you to move at your own pace, approaching each passage as a seasonal companion that you can visit and revisit as you need to. You can take the journey in the order we've offered, moving through the seasons from spring and back around again. Or you can start where you need to start.

No matter what you choose, the journey is yours to take.

With blessings and gratitude,

Jacqui & Andy

I

SPRING : BIRTH

❧ I ❧

The first signs of spring.
Life.
Where it begins.
Birth.
You.
A determined manifestation.
From thin air to you.
The magic and miracle of being sprung.
You were the size of a blueberry.
You weighed as much as an eyelash.
Buried like a seed underground.
Waiting to make your mark.
Born head first into purpose.
Born to bear weight.
Worthy of investment.
Worthy. Period.
Shift from Annual to Perennial.
Longevity and endurance.
Tending to your own soil.
Your own sun.
Your own dirt.

The venue to grow, provided.
The weather, provided.
The patience, provided.
The light, provided.
And within you. All your dirt. All your light. All your wisdom. All
your grit. All your grace.
All the priming.
The establishment of your roots.
You fought hard to get here.
Bloom.

.

1.1

Who were you the day you were born?

I.2

You were born to bear weight before you even knew how heavy it would become. You were built for this.

1.3

You used to be smaller than a blueberry and weighed less than an eyelash. Look at you now. What other miraculous things lie in wait within you?

I.4

What if you started exactly where you are? Not where you were, or where you want to be, but right here, right now, with the best of what you carry with you? The only guarantee life offers is this moment.

1.5

What makes a birthday different than any other day? The simple fact that we choose to stop and honor the moment. Counting from the minute of your birth, the earth has just completed another circuit around the great golden star that is our sun. And you are still alive. Still here. Still breathing. In a sense, every day is your birthday. Every moment is worth stopping to honor. What moment can you stop and honor right now?

1.6

One definition of forgiveness is to 'let go of debt.' What debts are you carrying? What hurts? What grievances? What judgments? And what if you forgave them?

1.7

You need only travel to a different place to see that most everything we believe looks different somewhere else. Language. Clothing. Food. Faith. All of it expressed a thousand different ways. We have almost as many ways of being in the world as there are people to live in it. Is there a part of your life that's ready to be expressed in a new way or seen from a new perspective?

1.8

What if you ended every day saying 'I did my best'? Even in the spring, not every tree blossoms. Not every flower blooms. But spring holds no regrets. It wastes no life force wondering 'what if?' Everything does its best and everything moves forward, opening, growing and forever changing. Just like you.

I.9

When difficult things happen in your life, instead of asking yourself 'why did this happen to me?' Ask yourself 'why did this happen FOR me?" This is not to dismiss the sting of grief but to limit the stronghold it puts on you. You can either wallow in it or grow from it. Those are really your only two choices. A spiritual person sees everyone and everything as a great teacher.

1.10

Try this. Wherever you think you came up short, say to yourself "I forgive you." Not meeting someone's expectations? Forgive. If you're trying like hell but just couldn't quite get there? Forgive. If you don't like your history? Forgive. If you don't love who you've become? Forgive. Don't waste your life force on a bunch of lost moments. Celebrate a new now. Forgive.

I.II

Sitting in the discomfort of the unanswered questions forces your soul to be resilient. From this murk your heart grows tough roots. Its branches are trust and faith.

1.12

You can't single handedly heal a heart whose complicated roots had absolutely nothing to do with you.

1.13

You have barely scratched the surface of what you are called to do.

1.14

Flowers don't look at each other in comparison. They just bloom.

1.15

Were we given the gift of life so we could suffocate it with responsibility and stress?

1.16

Nothing about you is broken.

I.17

The most intense love is born from life's mud.

❧ II ❧

SUMMER : YOUTH

❦ 2 ❦

The season of the blaring sun.
Windows down.
Salt. Sweat. Sunscreen. Freedom.
Fire.
Citronella.
The reprieve of a cold drink.
Breathing room. Boredom.
Vitamin D.
The constant daily practice & reminder of the sun.
Inspiration.
How she'll go up. Every day.
How she'll go down. Every night.
That feelings are not forever.
The only thing guaranteed is that all is temporary.
Focus on a light heart.
Take up space.
Have no plan. No clue.
Be bored, not busy.
Go outside.
Be humbled by heat.
Throw caution to the wind.

Wild child.
Away with influence.
Light infiltrating every single overworked cell in your body.
Light amplifying all of the things going right.
Inner fire strong.
No need to be afraid.
Align with Mother Nature.
No such thing as bigger picture.
Relief comes.
Feelings are freed.
Light shines unconditionally.
Warmth mothers.
Your song, renewed.

2.1

If it's true that we create each other, then who's creating you? And who are you creating?

2.2

Right now, someone in your life is on fire with love and joy. Maybe it's you. What does this joyful person have to teach you about living life?

2.3

Right now, someone in your life is hurting. Maybe it's you. What can you do to help honor their hurt and ease their suffering? And what does their perseverance in the face of hurt teach you about living life?

2.4

Human beings are born completely helpless. It takes us around sixteen years to develop adult-like levels of physical strength and mobility, and current neuroscience has us at twenty-five years for our brains to mature. Twenty-five years! A quarter of a century. If not for the people around us, we would never survive. Take a moment every day to thank someone who helped get you this far.

2.5

Let gratitude be known in your actions, not just in your words. What does gratitude in action look like in your life?

2.6

What if you just got out of your own way? Try not to give everything so much weight and see what happens. Explore, live & cultivate a light heart.

2.7

You are worthy of investigation. You are worth knowing.

2.8

Insecurity is like a foreign language to your soul. What would it be like to actually see yourself with no shortcomings?

2.9

Let your nerves have the kind of time where there is no responsibility to tend to. No expectation to be met. No debt to be paid. No imperfection that needs fixing. No fear that needs worry. Even if for just one precious moment.

2.10

Don't be afraid of the full range of yourself and don't be the one to stunt your own growth.

2.11

Hang out with a small child and you will be reminded of how easily you used to laugh, love people unconditionally and keep things simple. Hang out with a newborn and see how the one thing they become preoccupied with is light. Love, laughter and light are deeply in your roots. Children are not only beautiful teachers and reminders. They are mirrors.

2.12

Don't cut your confidence off at the knees because of someone else's insecurity.

2.13

Have honor, faith and gratitude for institutions and organizations that keep society alive, providing us with roads, water and energy. Have faith in the people who work in those institutions, providing us health care, education, and protection. Have faith in the ideas, theories and mechanics that make it possible for things like huge metal tubes that fly us all over the world. Have faith, really, in each other.

2.14

One of your greatest powers comes from being friendly and genuinely happy for others, truthfully. Your insecurity and your jealousy will bury you in your own darkness. You are the only one who stands to lose if this does not shift.

2.15

What really shows you someone's character is how they treat the people they don't think they need.

2.16

Holding yourself in higher regard requires the simple yet repeated effort of fully embracing and unconditionally loving a heart and soul trying to figure it all out.

2.17

Whenever you need to remember what's really important, go sit somewhere quiet and visualize the faces of the people you love.

2.18

There's more people who step up to the plate than drop the ball.

2.19

The sun doesn't choose who it shines on. It offers light to all, without conditions.

2.20

The answer is to proceed with humor.

❧ III ❧

FALL : GROWING UP

The labor. The fruit. The fruition.
The Hunter. The Gatherer.
The pieces fall.
Neighbors rally.
Community absorbs.
Hands go in the dirt.
The nurturing, abundant earth.
We break bread.
We feed off each other.
Leaves fall. The ground, uprooted.
Structure. School. Building skill.
Anticipating. Adapting. Developing.
Light to dark.
The art of returning.
The art of participating.
The art of falling back.
The changing of the guards.
The harvest.
Endurance. Patience.
Maturing.
Grow.

3.1

Listen just as loud as you talk.

3.2

What has your life made you a good teacher of?

3·3

Grit holding hands with grace. Courage holding hands with fear. Wisdom holding hands with doubt. This is the internal practice of the everyday warrior.

3 · 4

Let your nerves, brain, lungs & heart have the kind of time where there is no demand, no expectation to be met, no debt to be paid, no one to please, no pound to be lost and no responsibility to be upheld. Even if for just one minute. Freedom is always available.

3.5

Don't back something you don't believe in anymore. We hang in there way too long because of faded history and expired beliefs. What beliefs are you ready to retire?

3.6

Don't hold yourself hostage. Hold yourself in the palms of your own heart.

3·7

Let your presence be as loud as your words. When you are with others, hold them while you have them. What do people get when they are with you? And what do they lose when you leave?

3.8

Don't be afraid to give each other credit.

3 · 9

Become a better leader. Balance your work and family. Fine tune yourself to be a strong, lasting vessel. Hold yourself in high regard. The purpose of your life is to be of great service to the world.

3.10

If you live life for 'me me me' instead of for 'we we we' you'll always be missing the point.

3.11

Don't leave anyone out when you pray. Even the ones you're mad at.

3.12

Create a reserve of unconditional confidence within yourself. Combat all the influences that try to make you feel you are somehow unworthy. You are as worthy as any of us.

3.13

We've gotten real good at human thinking. Human doing. Human worrying. Human working. We want to make sure there's still enough room for human being.

3.14

Sometimes it seems like everyone's afraid, everything is falling apart, and what the hell can little old me do about it? But never forget: you do tremendous service for the world every time you help whoever's standing right in front of you, right here, right now.

3.15

How often do we try to tell someone else 'what's up' when we ourselves have no clue? It's only when we step confidently into uncertainty and admit our ignorance that we can truly proceed with an open mind and a compassionate heart.

3.16

Motivation and self-compassion emerge when you bravely visit the darkest corners of your soul and discover that you are nothing more and nothing less than totally human.

3.17

Some people just have a tough road to pave. It's hard to not want to give them the cliff notes, but unconditional love means meeting them exactly where they are. No judgement. No want for anything different. Just holding a hand as a listening friend, in sickness, in sadness, in madness, and in health.

3.18

It's very hard to watch someone else struggle. I usually soothe myself when I see or hear this by remembering that if you crack open a baby chick's shell, you will kill it. It will never have the struggle to build the strength it needs to live. People in crisis are just building some serious wingspan. There are no shortcuts.

IV

HURRICANE SEASON

❦ 4 ❦

Yet another shot.
A mark waiting to be made.
An unstoppable force. Applied pressure.
The wisdom of lives lived.
Perspective.
Hardship humbles.
The storms come for everyone. Nothing is personal.
Whirlwind.
Center of a spinning top.
Holding your own.
Widen your wingspan.
Have respect for the unknown.
The human condition will never let you let go of what people think.
Let go of what people think.
Tough love.
Time to unite with you.
Pray for others in the hurricane.
Watch empathy be born.
The wind. The stress. The contrast.
You are alive.
Live.

4.1

Always remember that even Mother Teresa had critics. Can you manage your fears and doubts and doubters and still go after exactly what you want? Still follow your dreams? Because if you keep waiting for the storm to end, you might never get anywhere.

4.2

No life event can define all of you. You're cut from a resilient cloth. Just keep putting one foot in front of the other. It's always calm in the eye.

4·3

If you don't own your fears, your fears will own you.

4·4

It's going to be a much harder road if your level of happiness is always measured by how your circumstances are going. True joy transcends all circumstance.

4.5

Great sorrow walks hand in hand with great resilience.

4.6

Rage, anger, anxiety and panic are just intense helplessness with no immediate solution. Searching for solutions, where there are none, is the primary ingredient in suffering.

4 · 7

Even the greatest spiritual teachers never navigated ideal conditions. Never. Their glory was achieved through the good old fashioned practice of daily effort.

4.8

Faith will get in the ditch with you. It refuses to allow you to make yourself small. No diagnosis can touch you, no life circumstance can define you. You're bigger than any of that.

4.9

A million things could have taken your life at this point and they haven't. Whatever created you continues to carry you.

4.10

Don't let uncertainty break your game. Keep walking with your nervous self. Keep walking with your scared self. Keep your rhythm, keep your stride. Don't sit in the misery of an unlived life.

4.11

Don't think for one second that your external circumstances unnerve your internal power.

4.12

Sometimes life changes so dramatically that you have no choice but to re-configure everything. Other times so quietly that, if you're not paying attention, you miss the moment altogether. But in every case, life is asking you to let something go. You can't change until you do. And if you don't choose to let go, life will choose for you.

4.13

Know that adversity is only testing commitment, building character, and strengthening resolve. Some roadblocks end up being life savers.

4.14

Maybe that pounding you feel in your heart is actually your spirit knocking on the other side of your skin, saying 'don't you dare think you can't handle this!'

4.15

Be your own air supply. Your own health insurance. Your own best friend. Stand at your own side.

4.16

Misery has enough company.

4.17

Being humbled is empathy's inspiration.

4.18

Pain is an inevitable part of growth. But it's up to you what you do with it. Will you let pain be a teacher? Or just another long, sad story?

4.19

One of the most important spaces to widen is the space between how you feel (especially when it's awful) and what you're going to do about it. It's in *that* space that your saving grace lives.

V

WINTER : LETTING GO

The Season of giving. Gathering. Hibernating.
Cold. Raw. Bare trees.
Indoors. Inward.
Longing. Ruminating. Reflecting. Regrouping.
Withdrawal. Self evaluation. Quiet.
A dull roar. Rallying.
Younger self surfacing.
Homing.
Steer the course
Reflect on purpose.
Slow down. Let your soul speak.
Listen and live with patience.
Steer the course.
Let silence encourage.
Snow falls. All flakes unique. All fall the same.
Nature in control.
Time suspended.
Hope gains ground.
Firmer ground established.
Freeze. Chill. Numb. Hunker.
Steer the course.

Develop the art of truly pausing. Pausing to not go to every fight, every insecurity or every doubt you're invited to. Pausing to be able to pray for people that normally you would not. Pausing to see the holy in each person even if they appear to be a holy, hot mess. Anger, irritation, resentment, lack of self support; all of it is a big, fat kick in the energetic pants. Be able to visit yourself for energy, compassion, and forgiveness, again and again and again. Commit to the art of standing on your own side for the rest of your days.

5.2

Each day brings us closer to the end. Therefore, love who you want. Feel the need to prove nothing. You don't have to live up to anyone's expectations. You have nothing to be ashamed of. When people get scared, they lash out at others. They feel threatened by the aspects of life that they don't understand. It's sad because we're not here long. Do you really want to smother the days you have left with fear and hate?

5.3

Naming your fears is the first step to letting them go. To name something is to begin to know it. To know something is to draw closer to it. And drawing closer is an act of intimacy that leaves little room for fear. So start there. Start with the name. Then move in.

5.4

Imagine you woke up this morning only to find out that yesterday, you died. Really imagine it. Everyone you know has mourned your passing. Every responsibility that once seemed to loom so large has been set down or passed on. Who would you see at your funeral? What would your obituary say? And, most importantly, what would you do next?

5.5

You can avoid danger your whole life. That doesn't change the fact that you're still going to end up dead.

5.6

Negative thinking is the equivalent of a pack of cigarettes. Your mind blackens, just like your lungs.

You can spend your days sitting in haunting questions of "What if?" or spend your days sitting in the healthy acknowledgement of "What if not?" The mental practice is the practice of not entertaining every fear that shows up.

5.8

The milestones we choose to mark on the road from birth to death tell the story of our life. Choose what matters to you. Choose what defines you. That's who you really are.

5.9

The same effort and energy we give to fleeing from fear could be used to gather our strength and face it.

5.10

There must be a time in your life where you truly accept that nothing needs to be different. That what you need to get is what you've already got. Let that be this time, right now.

5.11

Don't lie sick in a hospital bed and start to appreciate. Don't wait for a diagnosis or an injury to point out your blessings. Don't just be present. Be connected. Not one second of any of this is to be taken for granted and not one second of it should be given to the waste of complaining or to the insecurity of what other people think of you. You don't even have that kind of time.

5.12

To stand in the sun is to cast a shadow. The faster we run towards the light, the longer our shadow grows. Sometimes, the only choice is to turn and face it. To embrace it. To honor it as evidence that we are here, alive, standing in the light.

5.13

People-pleasing, self-doubt, and judging others are the equivalent of shoveling wet snow in an unrelenting blizzard.

5.14

You can't learn to sing by reading a book. You can't teach a kid how to swim in the classroom. You can't fall in love with nobody. Knowledge lives in your head. Wisdom lives in your whole self.

5.15

Most transformations don't happen because you are thinking about them. It's when we become quiet and allow for insight to surface on its own that the answers and directions reveal themselves. Don't lose the heart for the struggle, the waiting, the not being in control. At all.

5.16

Silence is the soul's opportunity to speak.

❧ VI ❧
SPRING : REBIRTH

※ 6 ※

Celebrate a new now.
Begin again.
And again.
And again.
Again.

6.1

All the great spiritual practices agree: the only way to enlightenment is head first into the human experience.

6.2

Think of a baby being born. Pushed out from the quiet warmth and darkness into a loud, bright world. Think how scary that must be. Then remember that baby was you. You were born once. You can be born again. But the only way out is through.

6.3

Every mapmaker who ever set out to chart the world didn't have a map. And so it is with life. The map of your life is made as you live it. Ask yourself: what journey has your life prepared you to begin? What is the map that only you can make?

6.4

Clinging to the past is like trying to cling to the mast of a flimsy sailboat in the midst of a storm. But rejecting the past, trying to live as if it never was, as if everything were a blank slate, might be just as foolish. Like trying to build a boat from scratch, without bothering to learn anything from the countless boat builders who came before us. Look to the past and learn. Then turn to the future and live.

6.5

If we can learn to increase our tolerance for discomfort and to master inconvenience, we can't help but reach the other side of our troubles with our commitment intact. We may discover the crosses we bear are really the fruits of all our labor.

6.6

Start again, exactly where you are. Not where you were, not where you want to be, but with who you are and what you've got. Just for today, stay focused on what's going right.

6.7

Get back to the wisdom you had before you were born. Get back to the wise, abundant soul who knows no judgment, who knows only unconditional love and who certainly knows forgiveness. That part of you that will always be tucked in the walls of your heart.

6.8

Be grateful for all shut doors. Consider yourself spared. The things that make you cry today may be wrapped in great joy tomorrow.

6.9

The most powerful stand against hate is letting people know that they belong. Including you.

6.10

When there is negativity we think things are not working out. Not always true. Sometimes it's just the right amount of tension to work you back towards path & purpose. A necessary "setback" to launch you back into alignment.

6.11

When making a shift, don't think about the mountain of effort it's going to take to keep your shift consistent. Don't look further than the day you're standing in. Doubt will talk you right out of change and keep you in holding patterns for fear of embarrassment or failure. Doubt harasses us until we decide there's no sense in shifting at all. It will then be impossible to disappoint anyone because the shift never started. What does your own doubt hold you back from doing?

6.12

You can care for others issues, but you don't have to carry them as your own.

6.13

What if you knew every detail of the life you were going to live? What if you could avoid all the dead ends, false starts and mistakes? Tempting, isn't it? But it doesn't work like that, and that's a blessing, not a curse. Because life would no longer be an act of creativity or discovery. Merely an act of transcription.

6.14

Everything you experience—including your dreams for the future and your memories of the past—you only ever experience it right now. Now is it. All there is. Now. Now. Now.

6.15

Use all of your strength, debt, sorrow, trouble and history as fuel. All of this can work to your advantage if you let it.

6.16

Underneath all of your fears, courage waits. Underneath all of your guilt, self forgiveness waits. Underneath all of your insecurities, great security waits. Underneath all of your denials and attachments, truth and wisdom wait. It's a matter of slowing down so they can break through the soil and come up for air.

6.17

A teacher speaks to you of her wisdom, but she cannot give it to you. Your wisdom is yours alone to find. Now is the time to go and seek it.

6.18

There is a doorway, right nearby, just out of sight. All you need to do is turn and walk through it. The rest of your life is waiting on the other side.

MIGRATIONS

LEAVE A REVIEW

Did you enjoy this meditative journey through the seasons of life?
If so, help us spread the word by leaving a review online!

bit.ly/migrations-leave-a-review

ABOUT THE AUTHORS

Jacqui Bonwell

Born on the South Shore of Massachusetts, Jacqui brings over fifteen years of teaching, studying and training in Yoga & meditation to this spiritual journal. One would think this has made her very calm and peaceful. Not the case. Jacqui is the definition of the human condition in the trenches of her own mind. Her two children keep her both in blinding states of love & regularly humbled. After graduating from the University of Rhode Island, spending over twenty years in Social Work and falling face first into Yoga, Jacqui has been seasoned by all aspects of life.

She has raised over $400,000 to support causes such as Yoga Reaches Out for Children's Hospital and the Homebase Program for Veterans of Mass General Hospital Boston. She regularly helps families in need & still considers herself a Social Worker by choice. She is a Motivational Speaker, ERYT-500hr, Yoga Alliance Continuing Ed. Provider, Director of the Sacred Seeds Yoga Schools, and the owner of the Canton Yoga Shala.

She considers anything that requires patience her teacher but she names: Rolf Gates, Johnny Gillespie, Pat Iyer, David Vendetti and her entire family (brothers, parents, relatives, friends, students, all of you reading this) as her inspiration, her support, her teachers. Her two children are her heart outside of her body. Her purpose in writing any of this is to still be able to Mother them on paper. Her husband, Eric, is the best decision she ever made. Jacqui thanks

Andy Cahill for being her wingman in all of this and merging to create this big love letter from our heart to yours.

www.jacquibonwellyoga.com
jacquibonwell@gmail.com

"I see you doing your best and that's the only lens I see through."
- Jacqui Bonwell

Andy Cahill

Andy Cahill is an author, musician, and personal transformation coach who excels at creating experiences that inspire people to dig deep, dream big, and do their greatest work. He's spent almost twenty years working in education, public service, and human development. The programs he's led and consulted on have reached thousands of people of all ages, from urban middle schools to corporate boardrooms, helping them build resilience, deepen mindfulness, and activate their full potential.

He earned his master's degree in education from the Harvard Graduate School of Education and his coaching certification with Integral Coaching Canada, one of the premier coach training schools in the world. He has been practicing meditation and mindful movement since 2007, and he is a certified yoga teacher, studying under the tutelage of Jacqui Bonwell, Erica Magro Cahill, Katie Beane, Stephen Cope, and Jason Magness. He is steeped in a variety of different disciplines, and his approach to teaching emphasizes patience, self-compassion, and a commitment to personal discovery. He is well-known for his capacity to bring the theory and practice of mindfulness to life with vibrancy.

mindfulcreative.coach
andy@mindfulcreative.coach

"We are all so much more capable than we give ourselves credit for."
- Andy Cahill